Dyson Russell

Marching
with a Broken
Shadow

The Complete
Anthological Collection

(✱) **green**hill
https://greenhillpublishing.com.au/

Russell, Dyson (author)

Marching with a Broken Shadow

ISBN 978-1-922957-87-0

POETRY

Typeset New Spirit 10/17

Cover photo by Bob Price - Pexels.com

Cover and book design by Green Hill Publishing

"Life is everything and nothing all at once"

Billy Corgan

Contents

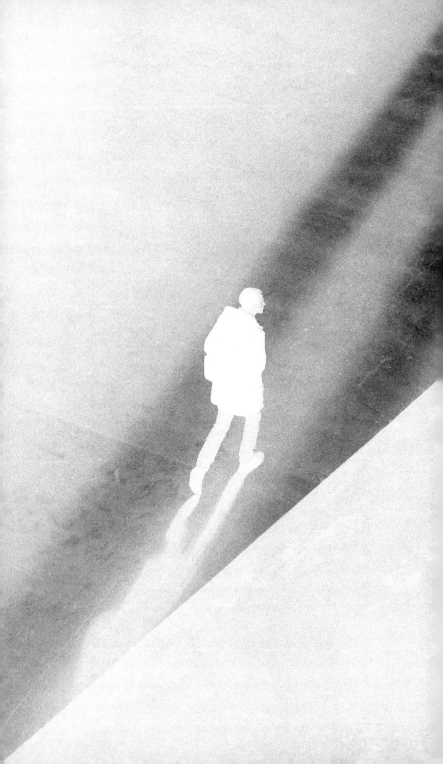

Tonight's Beginning

Sing
For your angel wings
And bring
All the pain you could surely –
Wait!
Tonight's not too late, for you
Open your eyes it's true
For the bleeding stars that grew
Into lightyears of warm glow
Will be watching –
Listening, for your voice to show
Where your eyes rivers flow
And your crystal tears know
Why they hide away
In the pockets of fears magic
Patiently waiting
For a moment to reveal
What languid words don't feel
But what laughter can heal
In its whimsical love song
So, sing
Feel the elements of spring
From your soft fingertips that own
Every touch they have sown
Like a glass river, serpentine
Feels the print of every rhyme
Painted in anguish and in beauty
– looking like blossoms in the candid night
So, let the words come to life
Like taking a knife
And bleeding these lines

To lovers in time
To the searchers unwind
Believe –
We'll come to know what our hearts can take
And read the words to how far we'll break...

Chasing the Hills

Baby eyes, look gainfully into pure sunshine
Autumn leaves laugh, immersed in the sublime
Decades to come, in memories waves
Past futures etched into hopeful faces brave

Teary eyes open, full from happy daydream
Hold tiny hands as we ride on the stars beam
Ticking clocks in imagination, time of nascent travels
The swaddling bands loosen, as baby unravels

Look around big eyes... see pleasant open fields
Taste the country fresh air, mirthful choruses, cartwheels
Playful sun chases moon, a serpent eats its own tail
With baby footsteps in mud, sun, thunder and hail

Close impatient tired senses, lids heavy on windows shy
Imperfect rain hits greener fields, in sleep bouncing
    memories spy
Dreamlands timeless quest, new worlds to explore
A kingdom, a palace, eyes that have seen it all before

Behind nascent eyes like treasure, pretty horses' stride
On this magic rainbow happy cherubs ride
To the hills so majestic, the wonder cures all
Archers for the sun, guarding on moonlight's call

And in the mind of a young cherub, eagerly growing his
   wings
A mother's voice mindfully plays, like the wind coolly sings
The words of divine comfort, like the ocean sprays the
   sand
Crafting paintings so mystical, spawning blood-stained
   notions so grand

And as that cherub marches on that rainbow, day by day
   growing strong
His quiet hands learn to write the words of his mother's
   favourite song
Knowing in mournful young heart, that as he learns these
   wills
His waiting legs will grow, and forever chase those hills

Apples and Oranges

As the eager sun of blissful impatience drifts freely with
    the wisest stars
And the loving moon of ages waves a loving hello in
    a voice that sings
A child starts his bygone crawl from mystic lands afar
Owning magic legs and incandescent angel wings

He lands in baron farmlands, in dusty paddocks great
And in a frozen breath begins to take his first steps
Teasing the ambivalent writers of capricious,
    enchanted fate
Writing with the most dolorous of ink, spawned from
    tears wept

In cocooned trees of emerald, he climbs too fast for day
Houses of solemn safety built from dust in mighty hands –
Words come to life and begin to bravely pave
A path that in bold writing, appears to be so grand

His mother leans in slowly, like the docking of
    gorgeous ships
Tucking this young cherub safely in his bed
A siren song leaving her lonely loving lips
And this is what she said

Dyson Russell

'My darling, the sun won't ever refuse to shine
The strongest mountains won't bow to violent wind
Your nascent eyes, your hair so fine
A body and soul that has never sinned

The clouds not selfish won't hold the fall
And the sea won't ever refuse to wave
In your little hands you can hold it all
Innocence the only way to be brave'

Apples are red in a baby's eye
Clocks don't tick like hearts do
For every dream that is a lie
Somewhere for someone one comes true

Climbing Trees, Love the Breeze

Climbing trees
Love the breeze –
Soothing softly in angelic hair
Curious fingertips pressed on sunlike shadow
Footsteps etched into perennial daydream
As questions overflow from a young mind in thought
Like an elegant sea becomes harsh on impulse
Driven by the chaos of moonlight tide
To row out in oceans, where monsters hide
In archaic wooden houses
Where fears provide
Access to forgotten memories –
Of ghosts that linger in lonesome stealth
Burdened by emptiness
And wasted years of prodigal wealth
Lost in the cyclones of youth
And spat out
More than once, by the friend in you
Thunder brusquely announces its arrival
Lightning chases the magic of survival
Just like the minds of children without concept of age –
Not knowing the journey that awaits
But forgiven are words scribed by dangerous fates
Watching on and painting new fears
Paddling on a splinted raft on rivers from tears
We've come too far to go back now
Music so silent it dances along
Fears, brave, future lovers write their song
You wouldn't expect it to end –

Oh, The People

Unfamiliar shadows in the corner
Nothing but a whisper
Cartoon faces emerge in slow shudder
Who's there this time?
See the alien figures walking
Painted faces talking
Musically laughing
Hold your young breath again
And they all say 'hi'
Oh, the people – strangers
Reflections in the sky
Stop mesmerising, dangers
The people –
This cherub chews it's sacred cheek
And suddenly feels weak
Spitting it out again
Never knowing to pretend
To know the oh
Oh... the people

Child of Eden

Child of Eden
Stand on the edge of these resplendent hills
Look over the greener fields, and salute to the musing
heavens –
Taste the warmth of dawns inviting call, and all that it
fulfills
The serenity of night break
And the choir of sun's rays
Daring blissfully to have faith in solitude
And in the knowing spirits
Where moonlight gifts a passage for free
In the summer
Walked in by the cleanest dreams
And in slumber
Wake to perfect screams
Of lungs filled with beauty
And gorgeous fears to embrace
Nightingale and fairy-tale
Lips red from the purest of fantasy
Two worlds in an eyes beam
And a leap of faith to start from
Reach for the sky
And learn to fly
It all can't wait!

Echoes at Sunset

Echo the strange songs
Of teary sunsets
Asking for permission
To be the moon
Write by the waves
Touch the daybreak
Of sunlight weeping
The tune

Untimed

Laughter yearns on windblow
Heard throughout this elegiac town
Our eyes stronger, in unison, in sound
Than the crashing down
Of blank stone walls, covering the fields
Patiently ignored
Not walked anymore, by free design
But we float above them in naked desire

And in a car park hidden among the trees
We taste the sweet summer breeze
Warm like coals lighting winter night
Hug the cold body, in stealth, in delight
And fright, for those who cast their eyes
On the frivolity we grow
From that laughter yearning
On joyous windblow

Touching Wings

Spiritedly naked in a burning flame
Tangled sensually within webs on fire
Angels playing golden harps glisten
And cherish the moment for silent prayers

Gushing oceans all around
Sing in symphony and love song
Humming to the tune of pleasant thoughts
And painting portraits across the mesmerised sands

Stories made within stars that bleed their colour
Plucked by a notion, caught in emotion
And written by the moon in luminous orbit
Across the galaxies in nervous light

To shine on the worlds, a glow too soon
The lazy but electric particles of dust
And the smouldering ashes caught in windstorm
Come alive and play along

As if they know why...

Nascent Love

Follow the rainbow
With giddy eyes
Spinning in circles
In ageless times
Heaven's halos
Never looked so divine
Painted in colour
Across loves grandest skies

Home From Home

Can you see my smile?
Painted across mirrors
Reflected in glowing ceilings
Of love... and divine questions
Stolen from dark shadows
Of lightless laughter
And laughter's light in sirens
And siren songs, sing...
Psalms, songs
Break us down, in smiling age
Beat us into dust, and dust we return
Dust like ash, and ash smouldering from flames
Flames and fires rage –
Home away from home
In straw houses patient wolves' watch
Spirits fly, in sky, for love of nascent touch
Flying with angels
But dropping like their wings
Every soul is innocent
Until life begins
But this is home now
Sweet cherub smile
Taste the salt of innocence –
This is home for a while

Tender Spiders Web

Muffling the naturistic sound of summer
Like the whimsical chirp of birds in breeze
Red apple noses sneezing on flowers teasing
Of the ache in freedoms groaning pleas

Hallucinatory gardens exude lustful pines
Naked feet blistered, and a mouth of bees
While poets leak their mournful lines
Like honey drips kindly, as if gushing seas

Resplendent rays tickle the serene dewy grass
And happy cherubs hum a chorus for belief
With rivers imprinted like hands on a glass
Waterfall's march to the liveliest streams

And as daybreak brushes over the dark of dawn
Trees come together in a swathe of green
Alive and emerald, like children they fawn
Of their lonely spirits weakness in dream

Light

Take your photograph in rays of light
Taste the salt of higher seas
Forgive up youthful blight

Discard your broken cherubs' wings
Laugh inside a voice that sings
And whistles like the wind in autumn leaves –
Daring the foliage to look like spring

In the glow of daydream sweet pebbles skip
On rivers calmly chasing heavens breeze
With striking minds and patient fingertips
The world listens softly as if set free

Red rosy cheeks and a sky bathed in blue
Bitterness in cracked hands that are no use
Filled up with the dust of dreams
That couldn't escape the tortured screams
Swallowed by the glistening moon in one fell swoop –

There's no such thing as nascent ground
All there is, is laughter's sound
Echoing the pleasures of sunny days
Waiting on the wind to say my name

Love

Half a bird in autumn air
With serenity in spring time
Folding nascent dreams of patient thoughts
Into pockets of deep blue mystery

A smile that fetches heartstrings
Plucked but never pulled before
By an angel that appeared from ashes
From fires that cleared them all

Rays of sunshine like fevers caught
Curious hands feel sombre burn
In a room filled with glorious magic
Who could know which heart takes its chance?

Dyson Russell

Gift Your Sympathy

Your love smells like sticky pine
Your breath tastes like spring air
Your raspy voice like stray paper
In my bleeding visions...

Fractured and faded
My now useless thoughts
In secret wars – won and lost
In my beating heart, in my tortured mind...

Air runs cold
And cold makes weak
Sincere thoughts of lust on repeat
The deepest mysteries of your naked fists

Memories of intertwined branches
Lushes and green in emerald and dreams
It's all in past tense
Your will breaks free

In dream catches
We run with pretty horses
Grow silver beards
And fall confused

All the old abuse
And my seven sisters in heaven
Marry my wet bliss
And carry my favourite song

Gift me your sympathy
In momentary death and me
Let's choke in tune
And glide in rainbow fevers

A sadness that is truth
And angels that fly
For all the orchids that froze
Love this rose! That bleeds on the dawn

Gift your sympathy
In loving memory, of me

Walking on Water's Waves

Sparks blindly traverse, and fly
Reflecting off scattered, bronze lights
From the most beautiful tears
In persevering sight

And sight is but a gift
Like a frozen window, in storm
Melting from glowing colour
Sparked by memory, and dreamed by dawn

Bled out across the dusty skies
Stars buzzing humbly like fireflies
Painting paradigms for stories
In the trust of open minds

The moonlight lets out blissful screams
Echoing on unmapped backstreets
That have never felt the patient feet
Of solemn travellers marching meekly

While the chorus sung by gushing river
Eclipses tortured notes in rust
And abides in words that say 'forgive her'
For walking on the water's waves

An Ageing Face of a
Mountain Lost in Violet Youth

In darkness –
Light teases shadows
Pens scrape the table
And dancers with arrows
Fire from friends bows
While magic voices of baritone
Call serenity in broken glass
And remind me of me...
Paperback – show off the gorgeous words
Words hidden in ghostly dreams
Dreams of fractured thoughts neglected
Neglected by lonely cherub screams
Moonlight glows like argument
While sirens tease
Of mistakes forgotten by naked bodies
And blissful violet streams
Running down elderly mountains
Never walked through by free
Design

Dyson Russell

Breaking the Path

A call to feel most
In a battle we unite
A struggle we felt
But a victory we held
Together we break blindness

Covering Future Tracks

I feel the touch of fate whispering on the future
Like a breeze bellows in sound only, at first
But then rushes over in haste
Masquerading as a patient whistle
Before becoming a paroxysm of howling wind

The moment the future becomes the present
How though?
Like a shadow not mine breaking my every stride
Or rain trickling down your tearless cheek
You feel but don't see, the touch of every drop that long
    ago dried

Sometimes we can sense the oncoming tide, or the
    impending fall
Where the still Earth shakes, and the safest footsteps
    still sink
Like trying to hear with deaf ears, from a silent call
Catharsis – or maybe it's reflection, swallowed, consumed
    in a blink
Of an eye that stares blindly at the antiquated wounds
    of nothing

Dyson Russell

A heart that falls in love with the pain of everything
A fragility that begs for forgiveness
But quickly forgets the hours, endless hours,
turned to days
Lying awake
In a pool of sweat

That all mean nothing in the end –
For no matter the tangibility of everything believed
Soil still comes to cover the imaginations of all
Once bereaved
And even the most powerful dream, will never predict
The horizon, in future

Celebrating the End of Age

You wait
Alone we stare
Fallen angels calling
Scream to me we fight for each other
Always

Dyson Russell

Guiltless Minds of Melting Guilt

The lazy wind of backstreets enchanted
Serpentine, as if moving to the tune of the breeze
Streetlights dance, and lover's chance
Is rolled like a dice on casino tables
The wisest trees sing along in voices familiar
Whistling as their autumn leaves turn gold
Golden like the colour of memory
Yet bronze like a memory rusted and aged
The moist green grass teases the serenity of the sky
Daring it to come down and walk on the tides
On the plains so fine, so synchronised –
As every footstep on wet cement ripples in wake
Like the most gorgeous ocean wave
Or the mountains wave, goodbye on a fleeting holiday
That seemed to last forever, but ended all the same –
The wind is painted in rainbow colours
As if the colours invent themselves and grow
Into the winds, and into the breeze
Into the heartstrings of lustful sorrow
Used by nascent fingertips
To fingerpaint across the night
Hoping that the wounded stars glow
Will guide the dreams just right

From Ashes to Dirt

From ashes to dirt
Curious fingers pressed in Earth
In bathing shade
And tortured youth
The dusty fields
They know you too

Like a fallen story
A never-ending charm
Terrified by its own beauty
Invisible in magic's arm

Written in crimson across mourning's cries
With ink borrowed from gloomy skies
And glowing in the pale light –

With sordid minds in gutters
Looking skyward to golden stars
Chanting to the bravest moon
And begging that it light the fearsome waves

Salt conviction touches shore
A reminder of perfection
In sadness, in bliss
Stolen from a line I never wrote
In a book never published
That's scar is all that is left

Brittle in its rust
Imagined by the day
Like seraphim's sling halos
At all who walk in fate

With spears at the ready
And shields coughed by rainbows
Swords clinking in fear, metallic and grated
From battles men never fought –

While dreamland reinvents itself
In patience, in stealth
Labyrinth of the heart, confused, but satisfied
Sleeping of the body, like night caught in dream
Owls play at midnight
And the clock ticks blindly
For no reason it would seem –

Shadows puppeteer, in silence
Bringing waterfalls to their knees
And spirits to find peace
Somewhere on their freeways that never end –

Winding roads, sunny plains
Prairies move with the days
As thoughts evoked become thin air
Drifting silently...
Forgotten only rarely
And remembered every so often
By innocence in nightmare

Candles light the night
Night sings to the breeze
Cooley swallowing the trees
And breathing in happy deliverance

While fingerprints paint rivers
And trinkets break into sentimentality's arms
Silvery beards mark the faces
Of the wise men who watch on

Dancing in frivolity, on the head of a nervous pin
Thrown sightlessly into a haystack
By a thimble used for sowing

Fabrics chequered and torn
Held together by their age
Like the dust in brittle bones
Is covered by scraping paint

Coloured like autumn leaves
That yell pervasively to the wind
Asking smarmily to be caught in drifts
Pleading with the sun to never lose colour

A bronze beauty cast in shade
Stumbling only where youth is wasted
Watched on from the highest ceilings
And chastised by the bravest stars

While prayers are sold to deaf ears
And Satan's in the lockets of our hearts

Pull onto sacred strings, for divine protection
Rigid like the web of a spider
Compasses lost in boyhood
Peter Pan for the wanderers

Seashells crushed on impact
By a howling blue sea
That once offered emancipation
To free the lonely souls

While boats touching rivers side
Sink only on the land
Through the mud traps disguised
As patient sand

Eyes closed, open, closed
Tears drip, fall, and dry
Lucifer lives in childish eye
Around the maypole
And into skies
Bleeding out future cries

In past restraints, in days unseen
In fears, in leers
In colourful screams
Blue and green
Emerald, like a rainforest
Tangled in the loss of bliss

In sickness, in breath
In hospital beds
Sirens call but never come
Ambulances crash into the sun
Beds burn on beaches
And spirits applaud loudly

Heavens open, revealing themselves
Following smiles on their way
While moonlight, the passage of yesterdays
Shines brightly –

And in the forgotten day of tomorrow
Lies the clandestine journey
And a soul not hollow
Follow, follow
And you will see
That painted rainbow will always be me
And the sky bathed in blanketing blue
Can be peeled back to show its true face
You.

Weep with the Breeze

Thoughtful trees
Standing inside hapless rain
Watching the perfect rise and fall
Bathed in shade and in shame

Laughing steam of hot daydream
Blanketing seeping nights in mist
The magic flower pulsating
In naked air and in fists

Clenched by the colour of token regret
Mud under feet, and ashes in hands
Grey, stars fade, into faces bereft
Intermittent in embarrassed glow

But left alone, by stars unknown
With lungs full of air
Like my sons last breath
In sorrowful despair, unchanged, and unkept

Rain flies away
Outliving thoughtful trees
But not before a merciless kingdom
Can weep with the breeze

Magic Flower

Jump magic flower!
Feel the fear caress
Leap for the ages
Scrape out your distress
For the last of its wisdom
The gatherers take rest
And sing ring a ring a rosy
In solemn ruby nights...

So, jump magic flower!
If your treasured mind dares you to
Reach for the most blistering sun
Call for the untangling of times truth
Minds of glazing frost
Equal like sordid hearts
Walk on fire with leopards
And taste the salty waters
Of lonely seas

You see what it becomes...
In particles of dust
In lost magic ash
As if it never was
Faith has no proof
Belief wasted youth
And dreams of rainbow worlds
Paint the nightmares grey

Poor magic flower...
Roots tangled in the dirt
Wings never grow
For the child left alone
In the bed across the hall
A dying figure weeps
Feeling every movement
As the soul seeps
Through the sickness of body

Angry magic flower
Trampled to dust
Swords once were held
Striking iron and sparking
Can any man walk this Earth
Without the memory of tears cried
The wicked tongues
The pen that won
To write the magic proof
Drowned by tears that were no use

Poppy Seed

Apologies!
Young poppy seed
Never meant to make you sleep
Dreamed a thousand years
Of serenity
With no reason why...
Cried
The tears of broken meek
Honesty
A named cursed by history
Memories
Make fun of the ghosts of the past
While the future asks the present
How long it has to last...
Walk between the clocks tick
Please young poppy seed
Find the entry to times truth –
Uncover the hidden ether
Fly back to what you once knew
Before you lost your wings
From the raptures of foul overdraft
In red skies and rusted paintings
With promises shattered by fearless speech
That never cursed the prayers made
In scraping shins, in bones that thin
Unbeknownst to you!
Your innocent words
The journey of poor birds
Flying into the sun
It's true...

Dyson Russell

Lion and the Lamb

You whispered in my ear
In blind daze on the clouds
Tasting the salt of tears
But gifting everything else
Once suppressed in laughter
- in stealth

And on the horizon glowing red
A reflection cast in skies
Yourself before you bled
Out your young blood
In exchange for eagle eyes

Like a flower on the hillside
Stares down on the careless town
But unable to take its chances
Is trampled
To mere dust on ground

And as you touch my neck
The hairs stand on end
It's a story I'd love to forget
And a love I'd forget to remember

For on that candle
That last light giving ember
Went out
From a trimmed wick
And a broken candle stick...

Can the lion ever laugh with the lamb?
A question one man asked
The very same man who caged their hearts

Youth Lost in Rain

Stumble in the rain
Marry pleasant fields
Laughter lost in days
With youth as a shield
Wasted on the young
But painted on the aged
Like a bronze autumn fall
Or a lyric on a page
That engulfs the warm feeling
Of nascent but learned eyes
Gifting the gift of magic
Stolen from the wise
But as youth fades in wrinkles
And memories abscond in fire
Wisdom becomes a curse
And childhood fervent desire

Dyson Russell

Ghost Ships

Swallowed were the mighty ships
Of timbers raw and innocent
On board the iron blades sparked blood
Spilling red, with lost thoughts hushed
Flags waved in gales spineless
Spotless sunsets dripped, diffused
Graves filled with shamefaced dirt
With idyllic grace and vanities mirth
Taking one more imprisoned soul
Into the watery underworld
- of yesterdays
Where friends ask dull questions
And the bows on girl's blazes
Whistle silently, unlaced in conquests
The moon barking orders at the waves
An ocean sycophantic in secret
It's true face hidden in rage
Clandestine in submission
Vociferous in punishment
Whispering it's will to the dark of the night...
So, see me for who I am
Cursed on a ghost ship
While dragons fight in sky
And spirits hedge their bets
On when the world will end
So please, take me as I am
Overlook the misdeeds of the cursed
And count the sins of the blessed –

Blood on Lips

Cracked lips, red like scarlet
Dry like a desert breeze
Sandpaper on grazed skin
Scraping like concrete –
With fires that blazed the past
Trickling into sunsets, in purple and musk
Flaming the way, for new day
Tomorrow a place for mist
Evergreen overflown
Tangents make their drift
In dolorous settings on the road
In strangers, in dangers
In scorched days to come
In windswept, in valleys
In futures succumb –

Dyson Russell

Fade into Shallow Ghosts

Leaves fall free
Like friends of mine
And stars reflect a curse
Of an ancient traveller
Who walked with a stopwatch
Ticking towards the colour of destiny

Swinging from his mystical pocket
The watch
Like the swing I'd swung from
In my most vivacious dreams

But now haunted by his ghost
The spirit rides the movement
Selling all its stories –
Bleeding on the highway
Like stains manifest

Stars shined brightly their naked beams
Like fireworks mesmerise childish eye –
But for every lost beam it seems
There are a thousand more lost wishes...
With deep blue ocean like regret
Feet marred by glass
And footprints left on sandy roads

Hanging from impervious bodies
Ghosts
Design how we arrive
With splinters to show off all that's walked through
Laughing wastefully
Until laughter runs dry

Youth wasted on unsympathetic children

Not the wise
Like the vulnerable sand waits for the dominant tide
Butterfly wings wet
Time abides
Never yielding –

Memories abscond, captured by air
So, the dreams can last forever
But never do –

Travels

Run to freedom fearless Earth
Taste the fortunes on fire
Mirth implanted in eagle's wings
Tides of gushing ocean desire
Birds fly to the tune of pervasive song
In sound, in ground, in all that's found
In the lonely spirit's tear –
Fall across the cracks of times sweetest fantasy
Drunk from the merry fountains of infancy
Stolid in the rock figure that made a memory too
But just like memories ended up beaten and broke
Into tiny particles of dust, and ash –
While mountains stand on tiptoes
Dancing, prancing, gleefully watching
As music moves their idle trance
Eternal flame lit twice
On a road not travelled
And travel in the footsteps of chance
Like a runway touched at dawn
By the most sympathetic of sunny rays
And an emblems ageing face
Just like new life is born
And cherub wings fall away –
There are no angels here
Only the laws of night and day
Of happiness and fear

Fearless Heart

What fearless heart
Torn and battered by fears
Dreams of memories in shattered monuments
That chased dragon's tails in grey skies

The clock ticks with blank face
And the sound of laughter
Like iron blades striking
With purity that calls lovers to arms

March to the stars
On the back of a solemn angel
Guided by the mistakes of his arrow
To rectify peace in heavens

And the lavender and cream
In tasteless, tasteful divine
Like a perfect smile
As dolorous as moonlight

Dyson Russell

Love x2

Ice cream cones
Roses, balloons
Laughter sounds
Like echoes to moons
And on tippy toes
At the crumbling fence
We stand in daydream
Please dream of me –

Dusty eyes
Fields and sunshine
Fingertips touch
Souls intertwine
Resting like autumn skies
Oh, to these eyes
Must I lie?

Innocence
Plays on the roof
Happenstance
Colours of truth
In a rainbow sky
That only she could make
My cloud rains –

Oh, the People, Now I Know the People

In the strangulating nettled thorns
You were born
Cherub –
Tasting metal
And swaying in trees
Touched by demons
And salty seas
In dreams, in beams
Of lightless light
- wounded stars bright
As bloodline trickles
And the eclipse in sight
Says the sun is burdened –
Rain flows, down it's back
Bitter and diffused
Soul marked and bruised
For lives on fire
And oh, the people they know!
And the dark figures lurch
Familiar in face
But the cheek tastes the same
In glowing innocence
Poison leaked by words
Honesty a holy grail
In a world full of birds
But very few doves
Gloves
Hiding the hands of shallow men
And the fingerprints of guilt
Cast and displayed on fragile ornaments

Breakable like hearts –
And within conversations
Of whispered paranoia
The guiltless spirits
Who's ashes burn the land
In particles of dust and grains of sand
Each atom a regret
From a former life
That begs once again
For a conscious mind
To say one sentence
"If only you'd known me when…"

Candle Light, Flicker

She stands in a candle
Whispers to her flame
Incandescent blue light
Covers her face

While hot wax drips like luminescent tears
In the fires crackle, the tears of lost years
And the smell of incense and demise –

Spells cast harshly from dusty books on forgotten shelves –
Dusty from the forgets of eternity
Eternity dusty from being left alone
Alone and unkept from minds that plainly forgot
That even raging fires don't burn forever

Stones
Replace the walls of sheet water
Heavy and blackened by the fires rage
Pixie dust scattered
Asking for unsuspecting magic to be graceful
In a show of whimsical fate
Flames flicker, wax wavers, pours
Faithless moors, the faithless mourn rivers cried
Lighting crashes, and stars collide
Bringing hapless but violent tides
While moonlight pleads for ghosts in night
- to show themselves
And ancient travellers howl to bring the past alive

Rainy windows touch a storm
Inside a dark room isolated by guitar sounds
Ink rushing like the blood of a fatality, but faded
Down the walls of poetry's lost paper

Translucent smoked glass gifts a passage of escape
To a room where men in leather coats drink wine
Plucking at fine gardens in daydream hallucinations
Confused by the enchanted dream of reality –
Reality laughing in the fractures of monuments moments
Moments pause on command if asked politely

Suddenly the still faces on everything
Metamorphose into sentient beings
Dancehalls invent themselves and sing
To the tune of gushing white rivers
That tell their story to sordid rocks
Impactful in their bruising wake
Gentle in the wisdom of what they've seen

All the while a song leaves the lonely lips
Of a journeyman who travels time
Sung softly like a breeze on trees
Coolly whistling past in peace
Asking the bronze autumn leaves
To keep their colour
While his hands that used to strum along
Are shackled in the chains grown from his song

Grown out from the bronze wishing tree
That stood naked in daybreak for all to see
Resplendent and mirthful, a quiet beauty
Teasing the dolorous passers-by –
The journeyman laughed
As the tree lied
Yet still he sings
The wishing tree won't run dry

In a solemn voice that stares down winters eye
Blizzards talk gainfully to one another
As mountains laugh sneeringly at the howls of the wind
The bark on the wisest trees pause to take note
And the angels reading emancipated put down their pens

Dreamland is broken
Sword's clink and clash
As leaves fall unspoken
And men dash free
Music hums to itself in silence
While the words of a deceitful tree
Live their own existence
And learn to be free
Skipped by a daydream if only rarely –
Like a patient storm refuses to break
Make a toast to it all for the night's sake
With flames painted across the roads
Wax still dripping on eternity's mask
Candle light glowing off its true face
Mine.

Blank

Warm like the wall of the sun
Heavy like the chains of the past
Eyelids pressed onto open eyes
So tired, dreaming of sleep
A great gift that alludes thee
Like a leaf that falls in winters breeze
Runs along the naked streets
Of hometowns lost in memories weeped...
No lights on to paint the sky
As darkness laughs
And serenity cries
The vengeful few who walk together
They sing songs and pull the threads
Of stitches stitched in time forever
Chequered and torn by the colour of regret
Tasted all along by hands with blisters
And watched in unison by eyes with tears
In mercury and nascent fears
Walk along with a candlestick
Where there are no lights
And friends are sick
A glass of wine
And a stained white sheet
Blankets cover the lost deceit
And blankets cover her eyes no sleep

Moonlight Shadow

In sordid sleep, I dream of sleep
Dream of rest
And days to weep
The clearest tears of happy dreams
In dreams, in fears
In days to rest
And believe, that rest will come

And in the dream
I fall again
Every haunting glance
Seems to pretend
That rest is but a happenstance
In fields of green
And shelves designed

Like a shadow basking in sunny glow
I don't know
If it's yours or mine

Falling In Love with Sleep

Do you remember how your eye lids wept
When you lay in sweat with evil in your bed
Your cleansed eyes burning, body unkept

Like your soul had left, and heart beat was dead
And even in your warmest dreams you're cold
Courage is human and it has been bled

Completely dry, and to Hades was sold
In exchange for torment, you're always awake
Stomached knotted, a journey so bold

Regardless of the position you make
You end up watching the blank ceiling above
The bed feeling like the depths of a lake

You realize that you have fallen in love
With sleep, while comfort is a place unknown
Like the beauty of the smiling sky above

The stomach feels like a river to a stone
Sweat slowly dripping as body restrains soul
So it won't escape the hurt it has sown

But it screams of the pain and burns like coal
Like fires still terrify the ashes of their ghost
Body and spirit congeal, reaching the goal

To express the pain and trauma they boast
Leaving the mind to question all once again
To cast memories of every suffering engrossed

Inciting guilt, posing questions, and then
Your mind becomes your biggest fear and worst foe
And unable to sleep you take your pen

And write the anguish of everything you know
A shy vulnerability that sleep loves
Unwittingly into slumber you go

Tired Dreams

In my dream, I dreamed a dream
A dream of rest, for restful eyes
Watched on spookily
Fawned –
The grey skies held
By blistered hands
Moving time
In shade, in shadows, in fallen rhymes
Choirs sing stories
Spiders crawl in arms
Of nervous men devoted
To bluffing who they are
Hold the air in colours
Sense your children's dreams
In a dream, a dream of a dream
A dream for restful eyes –
Rain drops hiding tears
And tears hiding scars
Scars but a memory
Of defiant battles lost
Amongst the tired
Tired dreams

Depression

Let them come
The monsters that smile
With dolphins that cry
In happy denial
They're under the bed
They're in my head
With a voice that sounds like my own
But a judgment alone
It's reason
I don't know

Dyson Russell

Walls of Insanity

Within walls of insanity
I age with the thoughts
That make me laugh
From memories obscene
A shrieking thrill
Sparks what I have seen
Through eyes of madness
And a smile from dust
Ashes of winter
And a sunbeam for lust
In treasured moments
In particles pretend
The silence of movements
That never end

Let me Sleep

Sad screaming voices
In incandescent ear
Murmurs talk back
Argumentative fear
Silence flees
Knows to escape
Whispers tease
For endless days
With weight of ceilings
Crashing down of patient stars
Impenetrable feelings
And a call to arms
Take your sword, lonely soldier
Take your burning flame
Hold your magic shield
Give up fear of depressive shame
Break on a stone
Inside a lion's heart
And capture your demons in a moment
Of peaceful sleep at last

Useless Thoughts in Oceans Filled with Nothing

Scenic ocean

Catch my smile

Wave your hand

At these hills

Where pastures green

Meet roads not seen

In a mind desperate

To see everything

To soon.

Whisper in a Voice That Only Spirits Know – The Loneliness of Voice Heard Through an Echo

My voice is hollow
No one hears the whispers
The spirits of tomorrow
Tangled in my fears
Of what's here today

What Difference We Find Between the Stolid Rocks at Lakes Bottom and the Sensual Path to Heavens Heaven

Do you know warmth like mothers' arms?
Like the golden oozing of treasured memory
The resplendence of the closest rainbow
Colours and pigmentations in fragile glow
In their sensual beauty, the miracles they show
Like mother's arms, and mother's heart –

Tainted nightmares of grave darkness
But free from harm in mother's arms
Freezing winds don't burn the lips
Protected by mother's fingertips
And all the forgotten dust aged on lost memories
Never congeal with the ashes in seas
From the fires of mother's heart

Though, it was broken from the start

But in the height of violent tidal waves
Mother's dying miracle saves
Not just the drowning boy
But his innocence and his favourite toy
Held in pure arms begging for mercy
From the vacant heart of merciless world

And if we all know all along
Why do we fake it so long?
Do we ever really go home?
Or are we just the heavy stone
Skipped on the empty lake
Because someone took a chance
But the stone finds nothing but dirt
Because our legs won't dance
On the water anymore...
And so, I ask this
Did I dream that kiss?
Was mother really there at all?

A Title Will Appear

Ravages of age
Or wisdom of youth
What did your father say to you?
That he learned too

He breathed red lightshows
I played with lasers
With guitar sounds and bones
And wishes alive

So, when do you become your own?
Your very own you
More than just an old man
That he was too

When do you start to love your stolen youth?
In wisdoms elderly and wrinkled hands
Of the man you never were
And he wasn't too

Footsteps of two sizes –
One for my foot and one for his fist
But the only laugh tastes like bee hives
And the coil of a sticky tongue around a mud trap
An old man younger than the child he never was
And a young man haunted by the ghost he will become
In the treasures of innocence and the burden of lust
What did your father say to you?
Before he became just
Another memory to fail to live up to
Too

Blind Expectations

When you walk down the pavement
And you see your shadow
Staring you in the face
No eyes to show the disenchantment you carry
But a reflection so heavy
It shows you enough
Run from the light
And into the darkness
Where there is no reflection
Eyes robbed of direction
Laughing loudly with blindness
As memories of kindness
Are submerged in visions
Of paranoid conversations
From those who sought to persecute you
And sit at the round table
With hatred burning red, and sadness so blue
Remember that fable
With your beautiful big teeth
Behind every image
Is a wolf

Soliloquy

Birds on the wind
Taillights spark roads, macabre

Clouds judgmental, and skies untold
Of the wakes untouched by burdened breeze
Watching on in patience and peace

So, let my soliloquy touch your heart
Like the wind that blows unafraid of the dark
Notes and words play along
But inside the soul I sing a song

Teasing the fortunes of stolen mirth
Blissful in innocence and awake in new birth
Frozen in teardrops that shatter on place
Lift the garments of dangerous fate
In muse, in dance, in solitude

Please oh darling,
See me for me

Dancing In Moonlight Tears

Sing me your tears
Laugh with this pen
If only I could
I would start over again

Let the good night decide
On what moonlight I'll ride
Cherish every dance
As we break with the wind

Oh, la, la, la, oh

Tree of Life

Tree of stars
Gift your kindred sympathy
Scattering forgiveness like golden foliage falls
With branches tamed like a patient sea
Lighthouses shine reminders of their marriage to the moon
And tell lonely men, conquering the dark, to learn their
    secrets
Talked about in whispers
And in crying tunes –
While a stolid rock figure, unpretentious
Sits beneath a solemn oak tree
Watching all the passes by
Trapped in mire, and forced to be free
For freedom is a curse
Sold by the wolves
Who have safely found prison
For their tortured souls...
Never imagined by an image sublime
Like snowflakes falling in deserts of sun
Or blackened ash sprinkled around trees that grow
In sun and snow
The wishing tree forbode, like a ghost
Made from a rope, and a sensual daydream –
Swing from that rope
Dare to be free...
But never forgive the freedom of being free –
Because home is where you start
And where it ends
In isolation.

Titanic Structures

Her sharp voice piercing
Like a needle through warm skin
Inspiring every doubt I've ever had
And forcing them to escape through burning sweat –
My scorched forehead, a symbol of panic
Dripping and warm
As if honey left in sun
Drenching my legs
And leaving me pale, like snow
Cold, like snow
Fervent, like windblow
On icy backroads...
Where every hour ticks faster than the last
And the heart questions why it chooses to stay
Don't be afraid?
My eyes only know one image to project
She stands at an open window
The wooden banisters shaping sporadically
Staring out into the depths of the ocean
As the moon lights the waves

Dyson Russell

Sailing Forbidden Seas

You couldn't survive in stealth
Tip toeing in the darkness
A clandestine movement so swift
A salt conviction so heartless
And I
I fell into the sea of shadows
Shadows without a face
Shadows impugned by witness
And I
I fell into the sea that swallows
Swallows every trait
A curse that's stronger than fate
You were an angel in light
But a serpent coiled around you
With a strangle hold
You were a lyric so bold
A song for every submissive man
Who holds an innocent hand
Who's hold on innocence is all he has
And the rain washes away all it greets
Whether in darkness or in light
The rain leaking on your white sheets
As you tip toe in an unwashed bed of delight

Loving Love for Loves Sake

You sprung like a daisy from the Earth
Cheerful and resplendent in your mirth
But bringing with you a fledgling curse
That quickly strangled my youthful heart
My fear of devotion, and yours to never be apart
You're like an ocean crashing against the sand
For every time you take my hand
You leave me wet and a little more broken
Your gushing tide like a cursed spell woken
Peacefully, I watch your waves so blue
As my sand has no choice but to have you

I once stood back from your waves that roar
Untouched like the bird that in the sky does soar
But my weak wings persuaded me to come down from
    the sky
And now wet, my paper wings, will never again fly high
My once love now insincere
Is the face of my fear
As I cry my last tear, with no surrounding peer
I will drown forever in your ocean so deep
And be with you for eternity in perennial sleep
For while you consume me, I cannot fight your wake
While I no longer love you, your heart I cannot break
And so it will be mine that is strangled, from your
    toxic heart
Your thrashing waves will take me to the grave
And we'll never be apart

Dyson Russell

Father, Father

I'll tell you stories Francesca
Close your eyes and dream
Of plentiful valleys in homeland
Where naked cherub's beam
And mad desires
Are locked in secrets
In towns where speech is deserted
And memories are never reached
Chains shackle the forbidden tongues
Of restless irresponsibility
And naked children dream
Of a nightmare that ends in sleep
To touch the warm bedsheets
Feel no impurity
Marked by a magic wand
And stolen from the free
Close your eyes Francesca
Believe as you in me
And see a world Francesca
Where father's just a dream

Burned like Lily

Lily, she calls me

From a blackened burned street

It's once orange glow

Dark in defeat

Streetlight marked

By broken glass

As her calls grow louder

But not loud enough

Dyson Russell

Magic Sold to Dragons Eyes

Smoke clouds laugh

From bored dragon's mouths

In ghoulish places

Forgotten by lonely words

With spiders lustfully crawling

Beneath worn out faded skin –

Magic for the mere trick of sleep

Demons clutching the nascent eyes

Of children too damaged to not believe

Belief is Where Disbelief Starts

In skewed thoughts
Of mindless walking –
Confusions broken footsteps
On patient wet cement
Lingering shadows cloud the air
And lustful darkness swallows the fair
Angel turned devil from whispers –
Forgotten moonlights torched eyes
Shines in conquest for hollowed believers
The stolid dusk asks questions to knowledgeable stars
As they fall to the ocean with grace
Touching the deepest regrets
Faces, skyward, look for what's left
A boy with a chain, and a dream
Walking on wet cement
Touching the forests of envy
As eclipses burn out in frustration
From hurt from ignorant demise
Laughter a music of consciousness
That deafens those that fight
In the street lights, in the dark nights
Walking and walking, without reason
With patience worn thin
From disbelief

Dyson Russell

Ephemeral Spirit

Spawned on a merit true
My hope to be taken away
Choice not yours to lose

Heartache

The polarising dawn sensually teases darkness
While the light of the sun gets lost on the seas
And within crumbling walls of madness in dream
Nascent skin touches pure bedsheets –
Laughter in bohemian hearts sets free
The rusted scars of eternity, in me
As she patiently says 'tell me everything'
And the moment of waiting becomes a speech

The Apple Tree Before Poison Ivy

Dearest soliloquy

Invite me to dream

My stale tears wasted

And fervent fears tasted

Like the rotting fruit of an apple tree

That once stood glowing, nascent and free

Blooming red innocence

Like cotton candy

Sickly sweet... invite me to dream!

My fruit has soured

My look dishevelled

My eyes in the mirror, I see what you see!

But I beg of thee...

Oh soliloquy – take a chance on me...

Please

Let me dream again

Poison Ivy

Poison Ivy
Like a car on backroads
In the stale windblow
Your angel face
But serpent tongue
Your gold hair
Seems to touch
The ghastly palaces of fairy-tales

And the ghostly moans
Fill days with fright
A mirthful death
Exudes sensual delight
Your wetness sinks in my despair
And poison ivy
You take me there

Razorblade

What a fearless face I see laughing
To the tune of Earth's slow spin
You have to walk in line
And lose your spine
Before your welcomes wear thin

And there's a darkness
In every street
As all the blind mice
Fall in love with a beat
That the pied piper never played

But me... well I always knew it
Cos I've loved loneliness
In a street that's bare
And faded concrete
Shows love so rare –
Sketched into the pavement
Like swans on a dirt lake
Circles of daydream, lost
And nightmares awake
In the dream train, of new dreams –

And I had a dream once
About my name on that concrete
It came alive, I went for a drive
And the song on the radio
Laughed at me

And fingers in wet cement
Were all but a fleeting moment
On that very crowded street
We all whispered
Whispered about each other

But we did it so discrete
That our eyes could never see
The betrayals
Our hearts wouldn't believe
But me, well I still know it

Because in that daydream
Loneliness sounds just like sympathy

Quiet the Memory

Darkness
While we're sleeping
Sunshine
Hits the window of dawn
Echoes
Souls are leaking
Remorseless
In an Earth filled with bones
In solemn shame
Touch the grace
Of your eyes
Never forget the seas
Rocking slowly...
Rainbows
Caught by the sky
Incense
Fills the spoiled nose
Essence
Vanilla and kind
Magically
Please bereave
Remember the way back home
In metal forest fields
Relics of disguise
Laughing in the fortunes
Of palpable demise
Be ashamed
Unless you meet
Your eyes
In tattered memories
Forget what you see
Behind me...

Magic in Eyes, Love Demise

Childish eye
Sparkles on the moonlight
Nascent trees
Growing to heaven in smiles
Daybreak raids the autumn of paradise
And sensual breeze, reminds you of me...
When the trees stood tall
When the land was just a notion
When the sea raged in perfect harmony
And the birds sung divine –
Your tongue wrapped around leftover leaves
Fallen, forgotten in bronze demise
The only taste the sticky pine
Poison like the soul that's lost...

Magic smokes, red like wine
Magic is your hand in mine
Rain down the back of a stolid sun
Torched so bright –
With linked hands we would run
You were a wildflower
I stood with you on the hillside
Nettled in the stringent clover
Bound by the laws of time
But you took your chance
With love and laughter
Dancing in rain
While I stayed the same

Now the hillside
The only friend of mine
Tortured leaves – with no beauty anymore

Dyson Russell

Daybreak fades, moonlight shades
This broken faith from its sadness –
Translucent droplets on water's window
Sparking mysteries and sorrow
Transcendental pleasures ask to be noticed
But once lost the mind is numb

The Only Sky Left

Far away lights
In ancient cities
Bringing demise
To skies
That once stood for beauty
An ageing dawn
And skyline, pretty
Mystifying and majestic –
Wonder tastes like fireflies
Daybreak fades, and the moon shades
Ascending, dark nights come to life
With so much distance between thoughts
Past and future, one and one
Ying and yang, and son with son
And sun –
Bleeding onto the lands so grand
Onto sand, wet from angel tears
Time only stops
When thought of time stops
Day moves, night comes
Presence burns
Like waiting hands
Touch open flames
Not for warmth
But to feel pain the same
As pain felt in youth
Fire in the sky
The only sky left
Is you

The Moon Holds Its Secrets, Be Like the Moon

Have you heard the song
Played by a man
Who sung to a crescent moon
He played his guitar
Sang to the stars
Begged for answers in his golden tune
But the moon stood silent
With dark glow and contempt
You're a singer of a simple songs
A poet's pen he said –
And then on he went...
Daybreak came, with sun and rise
And the man, his song
Had become his demise
His longing for answers had confused his heart
And the song he sang
Played again from the start

Sweet Memory

Slowly dripping
The paints not dry
Canvases align
In autumn time
Bronze in their magic
Wet in their dreams
Soliloquy of heavens
Paperback screams
Run to the light
Hide from the dark
Spread ashes in mud
Show off your mark
Tickle the rainbows
Splashed across the brush
And hear the song
Sung by winters plush
A tune hummed by deliverance
A song sung by words
Of the torching light of angels
That guide the passage home –
Carry back your sons
Sweet memory...
Reclaim your cherubs' wings –

Sunny Days

Sunny days –
Soft like cotton buds whisked across angelic faces
Warm like a tropical spring
Steaming against the placid bodies of virgins
Hot in serenity
Dragon's tails –
Like a moonlight toy, drifting around in circles and joy

Laughter in heaven's seven blue dreams
Touching the tortured ocean that sings
Flowing out into the depths of time
To marry innocence in naked rhyme
Stripped threadbare as archers take flight
Forever undone by chorus's delight...

Follow the smoke clouds
And realise the stars
Are forever in place watching who you are
Burning a thousand lightyears away
On show in the temporary time of day
What does that say?
That a burned-out star from long ago
Lifeless, breathless, and in deathly hallow
Can still be seen in the time of day
That exists with you and I the same...
Emitting a majestic glow, to show
That the beauty and wonder of once upon a time
Can still paint the night sky a colour sublime
And the memories of spirits lost to ash and dust
Can paint a rainbow with nothing but rust

Splendid white fairies
Dance in halls
Forever in tune with one and all
In whispers, in daydreams, in pleasant visions too
Oh, what it's like to be telling you
Of the unseen secrets of the very best tales
In particles, in parlance, in thunder and hail
Breath fragmented like stories young and old
Come together and beg to be told
Just like a song plays and takes us home
And curious flesh escapes the nascence of the bone –

Old pictures look just like a nightmare painted bleak
Dreamed in the most daring bodies of untrained envy
But woken by starlight just in time
Fearing the fear of feeling fear
But fearing more the fear of not fearing at all
Like tired wallpaper never erased
Glossed over by cracked paint
Gets laughed at by fate
In a dolorous love song
That once sang hallelujah
To a chorus written on the blankest page of words forbidden
With shards in the air
And nettles strangling clover bells...
Where paralysis marks the heavy eyes
Of wandering lost souls
Searching for sleep but never finding
The peacefulness of endless bliss
Or the perfect kiss
In night times daybreak
Tired of dreaming of rest

And restlessly waking to idle movement

Fish fly past the perfunctory betrayals
Of strangers promising their gifts from youth
Sold to the lie of staying young
And cashed by the quest to never age at all
But laughed at by the ghost that watches the fall
First from innocence, then from shame
Into the blessed ageing face
Of a man burdened by misery
As if his misery is all he has
Absconding from his youthful dreams
As if never dreamt
And in the mind of the flailing man once begging for youth
Lives the poison of a crises stricken old man begging for age
To give up responsibility
And become a child once more
Without the weight of futures
But with the whimsicality of hopelessness –

Loving memory
Dear memory
Line
Sensual in-depth touch
And anointed by oil
Fearful addiction and musk
Tomorrow's bleeding dusk
For yesterday's crying dawn
Moonlight forgotten in lightless time
And borrowed
Once again
By the blankest page of stolid stories
Sold in torture to the most desperate hearts
And told in sunny days...

Angel Wings Growing
as Memories Fade

Patiently caressing the whimsical sound of music
Eloping notes sing choruses to blind faith
And faith in fears displaced, like a child in a warzone
Anxiously waits

Bravery knows to escape
Escaping the stiffness of the rigidity
And mired body
Body and soul congeal in orbital mind

And the flowing wake of memories
- gushing from happy tears that remembered
Extinguishes raging fires of burning desires
As the mediative wind coolly brushes the past

Touching fingertips with the beauty of silence
At last, as smiles fade away
But the wet sensation of love remains
Burdened like lips cracked from the heat of sunny days

The shadow once poignantly cast
Now lives in shade
Waiting for a daylight friend
Forever made, the same

And in the perennial bliss and eternal paradise
Exists the ravens kiss, and bravery enticed
To whisper on the breeze of secrets
Travelling to the nevermore –

The marching spirit wakens
With tears in heavy eyes
Travelling softly with angel wings at last
To the place where dreams marry the past

Dyson Russell

Parsimonious Smiles

Every day the sun drips it's golden colour
Leaking through the wall of the placid sky
And I awake with a cringe
And a tear in my eye
As failure whistles on dawn's breeze

Some lazy stars still shine
Untouched and unburdened by the sun's slow rays –
My soporific body continuing to melt in dreams
And I start to walk in blindness again
Down a dimly lit path that shows the world in slumber
And the resting souls completely vulnerable
Watching each second that hastily passes
But that the sleeping never know they've lost

Within the fractures of the darkness
Lit temporarily by the bleeding sun's birth
All you can do is smile
Teach your face to hide its true face
Teach your lips to dismiss their colour
And I smile...
I smile for you
A smile untrue

And as daybreak wrestles with the half-seen moon
The fervent and oppressed run behind its wake
Floating seamlessly across the now burdened sky
Racing the truncated light of dayless days

With movements stale and eyes heavy like boulders
Sat atop mountains that forage their pathway to heaven

But still bow to the wind as it howls its direction
The fears of a narcotised army live in reality

The crescent moon occasionally shows off its beauty
As the sun hides away on whim
And the stolid ash travelling through the grey skies
Reminds all the passes by, of where they will end

All you can do is smile
Teach your eyes to love untruth
Teach your hands to hold all feeling
And I smile
I smile for you
A smile so blue

The naked heart exposed like a giddy daydream plays
While the road underneath broken wheels cracks further
And sunburned and blistered bodies
Scream and beg for their spirit to wrap around

The puffs of dust from ageing footsteps
Show the journey marched in congealed unison
But with blind fixation on the mesmerising skyline ahead
The transfixed minds never think to look back

Instead with hands that are gifted futility
And knuckles painted white like snow
The sweetest taste of defeat is tasted like nectar
And the vast rivers are allowed to grow

And at the aching of everyday
Like a childlike memory returns
All the vacant eyes stitched open
Are allowed to close in bliss

The stars bleed their torment proudly
While the sun waves a patient goodbye
And in the fearful daydream called reality
The wandering have the safety of sleep once more

Down a vacant path that teaches void eyes to smile
With the people who are completely vulnerable
And every second that passes
Won't ever be needed again

And as the ash floats loosely on the grey skies
I smile
Knowing I'll be happy in the end

Please Dawn, let me Come Home

The elegiac twinkle of lonely lights
Shine brightly on dawns welcoming make –
Blind faith has no place here
But still golden specs of dreamy dust fly...
The spoken movements in discarded dirt
Revisit the blissful wonder of daydream deliverance
And touch minds with heavens trusted stars
They sing a song that starts with the words –
'it's so easy, to guilt each soul on its way back out'
While deaf prayers of desperate sorrow
Cast stones along abandoned roads
And autumn shade rises
Teasing empty shadows
On their way back home –
Treasures become the rain on butterfly wings
Teasing each ghost that's left
And to whom the ocean coolly sings
On empty plains forged from songs free voice –
The brutal storm clouds
Refuse to rain
And frustrated roses with faces and thorns
Begin to chant for change
To perish is to vanquish in stolen truce
With the violet spirits that know the way
Back out for good.

Rainbows in Emerald Green

Tickling the sounds of laughter
Like the pure heart of a child
And a sensible mind of the aged
A time from yesterdays...

When sunlight shined down on sorrow
And bleeding dusk teased of a happy tomorrow
Lost in the dripping of night lit sky
Burdened, but sensual in its glowing eye
When memories went unquestioned
Like the distant light in dull passages
Walked through by curious minds
From fields denied, yet designed

By the fearful thoughts of their own desires

But now, where rainbows blanket the sky
In a colourful resignation
The lost treasures, once memories, only fly
To the backdrop of confused paintings
In sight

And delight, in mirthful choruses
Tasting just like sweet honey
Spilled from jars toyed with by cherubs
With serpents at the ready

With daydreams as long as trees in forests
Emerald green, yet lonely

A Look of Unsure

Teardrop laughing from crying eyes
Touch the windows that fight
For silent no's
Suppressed by laughter
The vanquished dreams
Of darkened seams
And arrows frail
In hearts of gold
Where hallows trail
Of pavements to unknown places
Bare feet walked on daggers edges
Alone and aching for home
In wilderness, in mist
In purple sunrise
In dawn, in dusk
In failures foreworn –
Dragon's tails dance to the sky
Magic flows, shows the way
That rainbows grow, in yesterdays
As friends forget their prevailing voices
In distant regret and stolen choices
Passed by the sun
By breezes that blow
Across nascent ground
In minds overthrown
Spirits on freeways blood their descent
Candles lit in fear
As passing torments repent
Their historical notions
Of forgotten lost

Black Light

Rendezvous!
Spirit on a mountain lonely, diffused
In the secrets locked in fallen minds
Ash burns to dust and carries the sins
Of all the gone who fell before –

Magic hides away from here
In voices of doubt in fear
In such a special place
Feel the rain!

And I've seen it all before
Within the most tortured moons and stars
I played along forever –

And I travelled alone
Exploded into the sea
And every sacred chord
Became a lost memory
And every single tear
That I had never cried
Is gone now... gone now...
And I'm gone with them

Within the lost times of day
Stands the mirage of one true God to pray
Mystical beings don't hide the demons
In the salt of the soul that you cry
Forget what they want!
Only one mirror will show the true face
That decides

Tears with the Moon

The virulent clouds dark
But the baby sky still blue
The wisest sun, it laughs
But with sensual light, the moon
Cries ceremoniously to the sound
Of bleeding stars in tune
Foraged millions of lightyears away
But here are the tears
Stolen from today

The River Echoes Silent Mist in a Daydream Named Chelsea

Echoes tease the tortured wind
Subtly beyond the tip toe of the breeze
Cool and sweet and on repeat
Whistling a sound that tastes like nectar
And looks just like a dream
Measured by a rainbow glow
That circles but never ends
Hairs stood frugally in defiance
On the necks of ancient trees
Wilfully moved by mother nature's impression –
Tropical green and lavender
Eucalyptus smell paints the air
Fires crackle in nightmares stolen
From the longest serving Earth
Ripples on the stream, like sparks in blood night
- scream and curse in voices unfamiliar
As the moon hides its most majestic side
Behind a mountain that promises to hold secrets –
The sun, somniferous, sleeps in yesterdays
All ahead of time in wait
And a scroll hidden beneath the dirt
Leaks the face of lost mirth
Across a friend named Chelsea –
She drifts on the lower dark lit streets
Of cities wasting away
While all along the watchtower
Sad trumpets talk in fear
Making trails of hidden notes
Lost in magic air
Everywhere around the spinning

And the over-hanging pictures

Fly the dust of fears

And ashes of evil

Pressing against the innocence of the ground

And soiling the depths of the land

Owl Singing

Fireflies play stars
And the moon plays along
Glissandra was her name
But she doesn't know it anymore
Because the pluck on spider's strings
Mark the pull on her rings
From angel fingertips
With touch of imprisoned notes
That pleased the fractured
But saved the foes
The lost fleeting
Forever a heart beating
If it ever did at all

Ripples on the lake
Hum as strangers pass
Unsure of their view
Laughing at their youth
To live out their promise
Of the truth
That youth runs dry –
A rug over the moon
Stars come together
Fireflies drop
As the owl sings at midnight

Only One Set of Footprints Marks the Shore

Fallen underneath times ravaged finger
Touch of prints marked by loss
Patterns, symbolic
Nascent but old
Wrinkled
Hair – dishevelled
Lonely like a stone
Heavy like a stone
Wasted like a stone
Who are you?

Shallow in the ageing darkness
Oceans tides swallow the submissive shore
Moonlight travels in burdensome focus
And ticking watches dare to glisten, for a moment even

You sold your youth too cheaply
Plucked your heartstrings in return for dirt
Tore off the legs of spiders spinning their webs
And let it all play out in fever like daydream
The wind picks up, slightly, ever so slightly
But carries the dust, and dirt, and ash, and mud
The elements that came to stand for lust, and us
And the particles that carry your still body without thoughts
It picks up again, slightly more this time
Even begins to sing in budding rhyme
And sing your name, in time with time
As it slows to sting your ageing face once more

Dyson Russell

The questions, the ones we all ask
They grow and flower like a rose on a tomb
Even more so when minds are stolen
And all that is left is the memory, but not your own

Without sentient mind to reason, or wonder
To voice in song or in simple answer
Dust and ash forever and after
In the sensual bliss of eternity, nothing

What lamb wanders in beautiful green fields
Do the stars forget their path, or yield
Gold wants currency
Silver a dawn

Guns play heaven
For children they mourn
Creation, elation, degradation, and spring
Doves and laughter can be a dangerous thing

With footsteps walked from a dream but forged
By a lonely stranger crossing the pew of the lord
But forgotten like a biblical principle
Is easily forgotten by the man proselytized

Paradisical heaven a dream of a dream, in dream
Mud and Earth
Memory, then none, name on a page
Then won, and done, and lost – finally lost

Could you believe this if you saw it true
Or would these words mean nothing to you
Would they lie to their page
Make a liar of their pen
Stories unravelled all over a gain

The strongest beliefs tortured

By the sound of suffering in silence

And the lord never walked

Never crossed that pew

Not with you, or me

Or us

It's true

Slingshot

The vast amount of time seeping through the clocks
    languid tick
Like a symphony in unison, blaming their notes on the
    frozen daylike sky
In the rivers lonely trickle and ripple on the wind, coolly
    escaping still eyes
Everywhere they go they see their smile and wave,
    watching stars bravely engraved
On the arks of a thousand stolid dreams, enchanted in
    mystic secrets
A harvest in winter snow –
Fairies play on the moon –
Soldiers tip toe for a battle of loves sacred echo, and a folly
    that has a name
Mirrors glance twice at the capricious notion of the
    disgrace left by men, in wait
Synthesis of the travelling serenade, blanketed by naked
    flames and fame and shame
Resist… persist… untimely shallow graves, touching dirt
    and dust and roots, flavoured the same
For a cure marked by lost tongues spoken by the words
    swimming in the dark
Swim on forever –
And when angels climb to you, friends will say goodbye
    with arrows
There's a slingshot you can use

Isolation

Drum beat hear my fractured thoughts
Pound away at what's lost
In the seeping minutes
Of hours passing
Only to know they're gone –

Magic sold to sleep at night
Stories told to drown the eyes
Woken by haunted passing notions
From nightmares built by lost devotions
Only to realise they're gone

Day break teasing sleepless memory
Darkness and ceilings
Cobwebs and screams
In the stolid thoughts that only
Know they have gone
But not to where they've gone

Grass growing pleasantly
In the glowing fields denied
Shells on sand
Miracles and beauty
Washed by gorgeous ocean tide
Painting the portraits of dreams but cried
Behind closed eyes –
In isolated thoughts of conscious design
They have gone... for good

Dyson Russell

Siren Soften

Siren, silence the nightmare
Marked in body and soul
Blind figures in dark houses
Rocks, lonely, are thrown...
Please, don't speak in footsteps...
Only worship the night!
Remember the days that we slept
For hours in our minds
Falling into slumber in autumn
Springs and fields – stunning reveals
And rains of chorus and bloom...
A sunny departure in tunes...
Whistling their naked blues...
In silence the nightmare consumes...
The lovers as friends who choose...
To chase the magic high but lose...
Their tender grip on reality
- diffused

Blessed and Gone

Hold onto bruising candle light
Lift your heavy naked mind
Drink from the friendly broken stream
That flows out –
To the places that warm memories sleep

In forgiven torments of tomorrow
The ghosts are frail, but they all know
What highway to haunt
Because they're blessed and gone

Temporal roses fall into pungent dirt
And dirt smears lifeless ash
Burnt orange black like anguished dust
Reminders of what's done in lust
Touching stealthy tigers in the night
Oh no...
The blessed are gone

Hollowed hearts and an empty trance
Marching together in soulless dance
Cherub, know my happenstance
This time around...

We will march to the fountains
The fountains of the deepest deep
Place your heart in chains
I'll prove I have the key

But don't follow me on the way to heaven

Footsteps get lost in celestial stars

Exploded into lonely moons and suns

The rust of tainted paths

Where souls are broken lost

And I am blessed and gone

Breath of a Thrill

Crashing down with blindness
Fists that never think twice
On a paper house
Built from magic cards
Blue with ghosts capturing the night
Walkways paved with mosaic rocks
Spiders' webs teasing every touch
Felt in tunnels leading nowhere
- but imagination sublime
Holding the wind and the lights
Every person smiling as they crawl
Across bygone portraits of stained glass
And patient sand –
From the shores of lost lands
And defects from ships macabre
Battles drowned out and so much blood lost
For the present of destroying the past
Flags wave silently upon the hill
White as an angel
Breath of a thrill

Camera Eye of Angelic Demise

Bronze sheet skin
Paint worn thin
Cracked and blistered
On the wooden décor
It scrapes like bones
It breaks like dirt
Dust in souls
And souls in Earth
Particles of memory
They fly around the moon
They fly with the wind
They fly with the tune
Of the humming bird singing
Calling the names
Of children in saffron
Playing escape

For far too long
The sun has shined
From darkened rooms
With speech denied
Ghost trains
And rain
Pouring in the fields
Tulips grow old
And magic swans yield
In the shells designed
By the shores rigid wake
In the dreams, in the seams
Of lonely heart break

Dozens of birds

Flock to the sky
Blessing lost innocence
To fast forward in time
In elements
In ether
In dangers too
I see a bleeding sky
And tomorrow with you

And in the nascent drum beat
Of a traveller's story, old
I hear the words spoken
From a lonely heart sold
To the inn keeper
To the pied piper
To the God that we see
Still, it reflects
What it was like to be me

Chemical Air

Patient moonlight calms the violent waves
Crashing irresistibly in the deepest oceans
Restless like a raging guilt
Yet futile like the qualms of lost frustrations

The boats at sea strangled by lust
Tarnished in their beauty
Reckless like thoughtless minds
Approach the scarred emotion
Of emotionless times

So, let us make a toast to the darkest fortunes
To the darling lanterns lost at sea
That remorselessly drowned the innocent soul
That once resembled me

Before I swallowed friend's magic
And breathed out stale air
All to chase the ephemeral feeling
Of masking blindness and dull despair

For the gift of sight is tainted
Forever haunted by what anguished eyes see
The capturing of faithful images a curse
In a memory built by me

And though the windows are gone
The enduring pictures remain
The skies never truly clear
And the hapless pouring rain
Never truly cleanses
The lasting sins

Of broken men
Who's broken sins
Are all they have left
Look into that cracked mirror –
What do I see?
The stories of a thousand faded regrets
An imprisoned man who never broke free

Here Comes a Wanted Man

Here he comes
The wanted man
Sprawling shadow like silhouette
Ghosting the day in the dawn of the sky
- friends he never met

In poison solitude
Like an angel dancing
He tells secrets
As secrets invent themselves in ash
Scraping dust from bones that left –

And the sound of mystery calls his ache
In the fractures of a spirit shallow
Painted across the ceiling in dolorous mist
Shallow, a fellow, who paints in red
With his fists

And all his life, he never had a chance
The crazy man just had to dance
On the head of a pin
With sprinkles of bliss
In darkness forbidden
With fragility of a kiss

The rocks tumbled down
And ashes on ground
Sang to the wind with fire in their eyes
In the dwindling backstreets
Just beaten pebbles
To admire –

And maybe time will tell
Why he has so much hell to sell –
Figures in fire like ageing companions
Spirits flying when lost and stranded

But the wanted man just dances
And smiles
As he makes toast to the darkest night

The End Days Rise

The end days rise
Awake dreary eyes
In middle winter time –
The touch of naked skin
Sensual
Like the warmth of laughter in memories
Yet lachrymose
Like the tears stained on notepads
With wet ink and faded lines...
The end days rise

Waterfall Daydream

Seraphim body
Naked skin in waterfalls
Blissful golden locks
Warm rock pools
Tingling on exterior
Freshness on the breeze
Boiling proudly from innocence
Into the warmth of lovely dream –
Then breaking into nightmare swirls
Hypnotized by gushing sounds
Blood trickling from lustful lips
Of the marching witnesses
- protesting stolen youth
Devil's pockets
And scissor tongues
Fish swim on land
Birds fly in the dark
You're not who you used to be
Before you breathed stale air
Lost plain sight from water's edge
And waterfall daydream

Cold Nights of Whimsical Nightmare

Cold nights and blankets
Pillows of frost
And snow fights –
Torn up by siphoned light
In daydreams of charcoal
In fires frozen by hearts
In leopards on mountains
Rainbows coughed by cherub's arms
Worship the false victims
Of stolen child abuse
Silver and gold and star beams
In stories long forgotten... not told

Crimson Roses

Frozen thoughts –
Body wasting away
Mangled by time
The time merely of day...
Sunshine abandoned
In place of dark rooms
Soliloquy of moments
Moonlight dooms
It creeps through the cracks
Of the holes in the wall
Like anxiety attacks
In the lonely spirits fall

Old Cemetery Road

Eyes wired open...

What do I do now?

Scream in fear for what I see

Speech knows not what the heart believes

Or do I listen?

Hear the whispered conversations of the walls

For sounds of silence are the loudest calls

And I can hear their fearful talk

There used to be a little girl in this room

But now her shadow just dances across the ceiling

As the boys in the backyard play

And now I am kneeling

Holding my hands in my hands

And seeing everything again

Eyes wired open

And there's nothing I can do now

I'm on old cemetery road

And it's a long walk home

Oceanus

As far as we float out
That's where I will drown
In waves of self-delusion
In oceans underground
To the sunsets edges
That's where my broken feet
Will walk on pleasant daydream
And float on naked breeze
To meet the smiling faces
That patiently wait for me there
With girls, and pearls, and lullabies
Sung softly in the whispered voice I knew
The voice of love, and warmth at night
In crashing waves
I lose my sight –
Without a fear in this whole world

Mystic River

Mystic river that winds
Through these ancient mountains
Seducing these naked hills
What reflection did you cast on me?
When my nascent eyes first met your glance
Because now although I see your wonder
The only wonder I see is escape

Mystic Mountain Tempt My Eyes

Mystic mountain
Enchanted river of my dreams
Looking on your proud green fields
This blind crusade almost seems
Worthwhile –
But the time spent is a while
The wait not what it's worth
And in the forgotten particles of tomorrow
Exists the stolen mirth
Of yesterday's memories sold too cheaply –
And the embers
From the fires burned in blaze
Tortured secrets forever unknown
Fond memories like smoke and haze

Garden of Eden

Last night I dreamed of the garden of Eden
I spoke to the Serpent
His tail in my hand
The only words I spoke:
'I understand'
Deceitful and evil we long not to be
Into the mirror
We choose not to see

HIM

Blazes of heavenly fire
Smoky fingers reach for the stars
Like a solemn tale told by a wizard
That flames poignantly in the dark

Magic particles fly in dust
And dust invents its fortunes –
Fortunes tasted by the bravest of fools
Wearing masks of courage
Stolen from the fearful

Spat inside crimson walls
The longing dragon of times stopwatch
Waking in solitude
Emancipated by dreams of a fallen world

With his daggered tail coiled in sleep
Unfurled like a flag waving on seas
He sits soberly, as blue as heaven
In the depths of hells land –

Tombs of the marked
Red like wine
Arms of envy and rusted scars
Touches of remembrance
And journeys lost
Dripping from regret
Dripping with remorse
And fearful talk
Of paranoid hallucinations
And sweat from fright
A daily chorus
Mirthful delight, replaced

In isolation and degradation
In tainted windows unseen
Magic loses its dream
When you can't wake up again –

Butterfly wings
Pinched in fingers
By dirty tips of unmagical disdain
Feeding cold hands
With a smile across the grey skies
And sunlight in the frozen eyes
Of the watching totem
Burdened by the miracles
Performed in terrified accident
And moons that stood still

Joyful verses leave lonely lips
Dying suns torch their desperate bright light
One last time, in beg of life
In a wishing well granting luck from charms
And truth of truth in lies
Watered down in murky tales
And captured by laughter's wake
Weeping in lonesomeness
For forever's lost wave

Happiness?
Deft touch, and hold back –
Arms of spiders
Lucklessness in faint eye shadow
Dresses wave in the gleeful wind
As strings blow on the gutters
Plucked from the greatest fears
In a mind once imagined...

Dare a stone heart to beat
It can't break in peace
But can sink in the river
Of tears cried for never beating
Like an ode to cruelty

Halos shine in platinum
Teasing the evil flowers on the hillside
Where mercy questions boldness
And boldness looks like a face you see
In rivers reflection –

Nascent dreams
Of discourse invented in wartime struggle
And rain, and thunder, and lightning
Pale, like the footsteps taken in chase
Of a dream imagined by waiting
For the moment to be right
And the ending to come
Before the beginning of the journey
Walk, run, crawl on your knees
Time will laugh in mountains and soil
Their faces marked by the river

For when the lost sons
March through the skies
They dodge the fallen stars
And the wise
Too intelligent to elope one last time
Too attached to let go of the prospering sky
Like a newborn child holding onto mothers' breast
As a boy fallen from her chest
Hanging on to youthful irresponsibility
But blessed

By the wisdom to carry on
In pain

Serpents laugh in the backstreets of trauma
As newborn vampires kiss the memories of cold skin
Moonlight man laughs in tune with dead stars
As shadows play together
And the spiders in guitars
Pierce the flesh of the wandering songs of travel

Yesterdays...
Poison girls, like a poison heart
Of a tomorrow that never comes
The tears once forgotten
Buried alive by love
In younger arms –

Breath fogs the cracked window
Creating messages so thoughtfully written
But written out of hot breath from fear
In forbidden torments
And cold hands that feel everything

In his withered ghost
The explication of judgment alone
That can never weep long enough
For the salty conviction of lost and painful tears
To stain the tongues
That taste these fears
And they all know –
Silent prayers fall on deaf ears
Tombs will flower
But in winter years
Wither like his ghost

Snowflakes carved in beauties image
Turn to spring to show off their glow
And glaciers melting beneath nervous feet
Wash into the roaring seas
Like the time of a soul
Taken too early
Washes into forgotten places
Sleeping eyes never know they've lost
But the eyes on friends faces
Show the cost

Lashes become ashes
Windows but dust
Wounds count their blessings
And deride in rust
Souls peel back their bandages
And water their bourgeoning scars –

The wrath of a malevolent god
- impossible
Without the sin of a blessed angel
Resting, the carcass of eternity laughs
In the face of eternal waste
Tasting the raw flesh of virgins
That escapes the wretched scent of blame
In bottles of shame
Deceived by spirits treacherous
And laughed at finally
By the secrets disappeared into the wind –

Lonely Planet

Silver planet in night sky
Strange unchained direction
Like drunken feet on a staircase
On the hills –

Plead with prayers to the mud traps
On the nascent plains, and pale mind
Gushing waters
Translucent
Aqua even
Murky in the colour of resignation
And the texture of forgotten freedom

Water as a friend called Neil –
Touch the fabric of the land
And then treat it like a presence
Of an old friend lost in stars

That regimented orbit
Could you even call it?
Like a sea of lustful kisses
Circulate with waves
Splashing naked bodies
And lingering
Long after lips but dry
And crack in strong winds

The path not often take by buffalo
But walked on by magic
In a spell...
And in the ageless motion picture
Called the field
Through skies eyes
It's still a spell

Simple Stories

Faithless child
Hold onto your sweet December smile
Wrap your nascent arms around summers breeze

Pull up fervent oars from patient rivers crossed
The hearts lost
In fields of serenity
And in the season of eternity
Naked cherubs beam

Magic – like the electric glow of warmth from love –
Will set you free as the dove flies in skies so peaceful
Spells bind the frail, with teardrops a grail
Like the most reverent arks set sail
On the fateful sympathetic winds

As golden spiders' webs pull the stars bleeding light
And submit to the moons sensual tug on gushing ocean
    waves
The greenest pastures designed by ageless times
Caress the minds of sighs on the dripping horizons

And the wounded autumn skies tell truth in lies
With daydream trickling down the wall of the sun
Marked by desperation to love everyone

Bleeding Autumn Skies

Our solitude a coveted emancipation
Loneliness withers in autumn skies
'Together' a notion of our creation
Free from springs collective sighs
Axioms forgotten no longer a chance
Aptitude returns to once again sustain
Our minds face defeat, body unknown
A love not taken and the devil will dance
Unity unfathomable but without it such pain
For it's when we're together we're truly alone

Dyson Russell

Real Love

Polished green eyes
A simple scar
The wildflowers tease
The hillside they're on
Flying on the breeze
To the backdrop of dawn
Red like blood
From the selfless sky
Inside a dream
Of naked desire
Within the crevasses
Of dark sensual oceans
Into the stinging depth
Of selfish emotions
It's real love this time –
In seasons, in dirt
Musk blowing teardrops
In magical hurt
With thickness of wine
And scattered in dust
Of strangers won
To love of lust

The World's Fair

Treasure the open plains
So tastefully green and fair
Angelic faces beaming brightly
Golden locks and wavy hair
Merry-go-rounds spinning
And prancing ponies there
It's all to see
At the world's fair
Happy faces in shooting stars
Children with magical dust playing
Laughing proudly with kindness
Touching Excalibur
Dragon slaying –
Magic is real
Just let yourself feel
The gift of youth
And the love of you
Feel the truth
Of happiness
In the world's fair...

Dyson Russell

Graceful Love Like a Swan

Like a daring moth
In the darkest skies
Seeking out a naked flame

I caught a glance
Of your teary eyes
Staring at mine
Just the same

In that fleeting second
A moments heartbeat
I felt your tortures
For eternity
And fell in love with you

Your sadness like raindrops
My flower on hilltops
Wet and stained from your impression

And my love like a bleeding star
Oozing magic from afar
Light years away
But in full view
Close enough to touch

With dusty fingerprints
And gorgeous clapping hands
Hoping to hold the moment
And never let it end

But when it did –
I wrote these words
And you dreamed vivacious dreams

Guided by graceful swans
Etched in glorious memory
It seems...

Dawa

What pleasant daydreams
Do you hope to never wake from?
What silent fear
Is always gone?

What peace is hope?
Where does strength run from?
When you go to the lake
But the lake is dry

I'll sooth your rusted scars
If you fall asleep next to me
I'll show you mine, and sooth them too –

And one day take a chance
Maybe our hearts can dance...

Graceful songs
Will greet our patient ears, taught
To never sing in blind faith
And the dancehalls
That once lurked chilling shadows
Will come alive
And set you free

I'll love your sadness, angel
If you sing to me in calming voice
I'll sing along, just you see!

Let our broken hearts set sail
Even with our wounded voices, frail
We can guide this sinking ship
Home at last –

What were the words
That sent you to paradisical heaven
What were the songs
That made you smile?
Who cares now –
I'll belong, in song with you

Tears can bring you home, it's true
And I'll cry for you

If you want me too...

Cherub's Harps

The darling words of songs in tune
Play like cherub's harps
On the most beautiful humming breeze

Gorgeous words, lyrical and sweet
Touching with sensuality
Bones that never felt free

Close your eyes
Tears inside
The books burn in a haze

And the ash remembers lost days
When night came, and silence rained
Rained down from night sky

Dark, and starry, and forgotten in time
Like a pleasant daydream
You wish was true

But the dream has no choice
But to have you...

Through Blind Eyes

You laugh at your reflection
And cry at your eyes
Holding your mirror above the skies
Showing me all of this worlds lies
But tilting it slightly so I too can see
Just how majestic the truth can be

Dyson Russell

I am Lighting I am Thunder

Crescent moon
Did you see the falling tear drops?
Leaking through the patient roof
I once knew as home
In a plentiful journey, blue
Where the cracks on aged concrete
Knew my name
And all along the dusty plains
I ran
In search of yesterday
Forbidden by tomorrow
To make the same mistakes
Like lightning crashing in solitude
Emancipated from thunders roar
Striking with innocence and damage unspoken
Just like in days before
But the patience of learning falls flat in the sky
And in its incandescent beauty and danger
I realise that I
Am just like that crash of light
Like the thunder startling gleefully
And the crescent moonlight –
For the strength is always there
The power and pretty, too
Just as it is for all
As it is for you
But just like that thunder and lighting
Like a tree wrapped in stolid bark
The majestic glow of resilient wonder
Shows most poignantly in the dark

White Horses

There's a place beyond the fog of fog
In the bleeding heart of winter
Where magic drips from viewless treetops
And suns freeze mesmerised by day

The breeze stings like rusted sheet wire
And heartache tastes like sand
Happenstance feels like a cosy dust storm
Bathing stolid cheeks in salty tears

Rainbows choose their own colour in unison
As white horses run on gorgeous hillsides
Exuding playful daydreams
For all who see this golden paradise

It's a place where eyes connect to souls
Where fingertips touch in shiver
Where words echo to the sound of laughter
Saying over and over

That you can only be you –
White horses making tears in the rain
You can only be you
My love.

Lonesome Nights

If you could see such tenderness
You would cry for a thousand summers
Winter would look like oceans
And lovers silently devoted
Would show their emotions
And give away their spell
Silent fog would dimmer
And in the darkness forgive her
For the story never lasts

Watcher

Hear patiently a fairy-tale
Down in a mild summer street
Mrs. Clarke loves conversation
With wavy hair and ice cream

She touches an empty bottle in dim light
Her father dances and sings
While her brother plays lonesome guitar sounds
Mrs. Clarke plays with her rings

She suddenly has twinkle in her eye
I wish I could follow to her soul
Stand up in scorching moonlight
Show off some of that nascent glow

Pass me the bottle of whiskey, Mrs. Clarke
I want to be someone with you
Somewhere, somehow
Believe in me, through me
Stare right back at me...

Catch a glance of night sky ceiling
Rainbow colours painted with tears
See our faces dripping from the colours
Symbolic, like colours we drip

And if you knew me Mrs. Clarke
I would watch you take a sip
From that empty bottle
Dimly in blackened light

You'd see right through me
As my ghost stares back at me

Dyson Russell

Memory of Bygone Choices

When a bygone moment becomes a memory to hold
Like a duckling in hands of the most patient children
Or stories wilfully told
To sleeping beauties in the grey nights
Then, wake to a sunbeam
Cast on pleasant times and magic...

Fall into the ocean's hair
Touch the lily of despair
I needed someone
To hold needlessly
With trinkets on lonesome paths
And salted surreptitious dreams

In love majestic as a rainbow
Flowed in silence by rivers calming breeze
That needed someone
Like I begged for you...

But one day the wind will change
And tears will fall like rain on dusty windshields
Powder in our veins
And Satan in the manger of our hearts

Dust turns to dark
With blood from the impervious cuts
Of eternity –

Chased unwillingly by autumn day
Fair and rare amongst the trees
Eloping with bronze and graceful leaves
Just like we leave it all behind
For dreams, it seems

A naked heart
And a scorched soul, riding a sunset
That takes your childlike breath away –

From the day I chose you
I knew the sky blue
Would fall into the ocean
And the ocean so fearful
Would curl itself into a ball
And fall unwittingly
Too.

Into Night Scars

Waiting in solitude
As time blankly ticks
Darting eyes impatient
Matched only by the clock's hands
Rain hits the rusted roof above
Laughing on impact at its boldness
And coldness, in sensual chill
Fears leaking through rough exterior
Dripping a colourful resignation
And protection from freedom
Catharsis – tastes like a fairy-tale
And canonical stories sound like dust
Caught in the winds, misdirected
Laughed at by whirlpools, unaffected
By the stain of debris on their pure reflection –
And memories seem to burn
Like a fire trapped in a candle
As the loss of friends is questioned
Like a strange thought in woken daydream
You never know you had

Tears flow freely
As if knowing they'll never run dry
The cheeks forever stained
By the memory of lost tears
Wept for reasons forgotten
But that the heart could never forget

And even on the bleeding dawn
Strange clouds still mark the sky
All imperfect, yet flying forward
Unfazed by the simplicity of their impression
Ignorant to the audience that questions their drift
But can only dream of creating a wake so untouchable

And from these clouds, still rain pours
The same, yet different each time
Until you cry so many tears that the rain turns dry
And reveal so many fears
You can stop living scared...
Don't worry little moth
The flame will come to you

Paperback Shadow

The itching of your pen as you write your poems
The sound of the keys as I sing my lonesome notes
All we see are our shadows across the wall
Not knowing what it's like to share our homes

My lyrics must cry when they hear their noise
Your words must beg for a happier voice
But our reflections are mired in our paper so crinkled
That we no longer have a choice

Astral Planes

Far away lights
Splinter across the water
Fetching light glows for wasteful men on wasteful boats
Daddy laughs
And the sun and son watch on in unison
Both without a chance
Paperback scrolls mammas hidden poems
The life she lost
When she married fortune
And sold her soul away
Like a needle in a haystack laughs at fading paint
And the seeping astral plans...
Universe crying
Tears of days
From fame
From shame
In shadows
In whispers
The grass still grows
But the green is tinged brown
And on this side of town
We live in concrete
The lover's arks
Fade in the dark
Glowing only the taste of hubris
Lonely words
And rosy songs
As the boat docks
But fades in the astral planes

Shutter

Does your whisper still linger
Inside these walls
Or is the voice in my head
Simply yours –
A lonely cry
And defeated ocean waves
That flow to paradise
We arrived at in yesterdays
The voices hum mournfully
Silence dethrones the shade
But in the corner of my room
Your shadow still stays

Fallen Angel

A fallen angel you call out
Singing to the charms of the lost

With a familiar voice
And resplendent glow
Imploring safety in the darkest night –

But the voice isn't yours
It's but an echo
Of the calling of a name marked by time

The River

At the bottom of the murky river
Is where I calmly sit
Waiting for my mirror
To crack into tiny pieces
Reflecting the once youthful light
Bouncing in my exhausted thoughts
Every past memory
Of ages wrinkled and paused
Showing each bygone moment
That lasted for eternity
But now that eternity is over
I wish for a little more...

Anonymous

Last remains –
Flags of aroma waved
From night born touch
Bound for dust
Hills say
'Run from
A cheap funeral and a grave'
Impatient I remain
Standing in the pouring rain
Reading out a eulogy
I wrote for myself
Marching to heaven
With wings built in stealth

Wishing Well Dry

Spirit behind my eyes
The ghost that I can't see
Whispering on daydream
In a voice of serenity

It moves with patient wind
Slowly like a shallow scream
That echoes and shatters on impact
In the darkness beneath
The ether –

My tired body once lived
In the days of plentiful sunshine
Where laughter was rich medicine
And youthful pockets were filled with life
While sickness was a cure
In beds of pale white
But now we dream of days
Where it's all alright
Forever in light –
Tears on the glass
Translucent and dripping
The smiles of past
Lost in the sky
Spirit please
Invite me to dream
Swim with failed men
In this wishing well
That's dry

The Fields won't Dry as the Memories Deride, but the Guilt a Tide in an Ocean so Great

Wrinkled skin and a lonely tear drop

Faded, yellowing

Broken at last

Spoken at last

Token and tokenistic

The heaviness in the eyelids and heart

Waves of gushing regret

Fields of wasted guilt

Mown to nothing by poison

But the growth returns each time

And the silky swathes blanketing rage

Making the conscience boiling hot

The pain dripping through exterior

Sweat profusely pouring

An age calling

At dawn

For the crying memory, torn

You can't take back the past

The future burdened by regret

Regret touched like fingers on glass

The print will always be there

And when the bottle shatters and breaks

That print will still be there

The City Cries from Rivers Light

Rusted cheeks
Burned in grace by teardrops
Aged like a tin roof
And aged like rusted scars

Burdened arms
Wrapped around an innocent thought
Dreamed of in a nightmare so long before
Only a shadow
Of the name I once knew...

The rivers, they've dried
- I'll miss you tonight
And though I have the lanterns light
These city streets I once called home
Still haunt me through the calm of my bones –

Ghost in my skin
Song on my lips
Revered like a mystic child
Hopeless but sacred
Cherub, angelic but naked
A sign of the power
Of rudimentary goodness
And the quest to lose it all –

In the winding backroads
And spooky windblows
Fingers cracked and hands of dust
I wait for your soul to touch;
Mine... as the radio plays...

I miss you each night –
But when I drown and survive
You can relive everything...
And if you wait, maybe fate
Will dry the water once more

But still the city walks –
Its aching bones hurting with every stride
I strip my soul down to nothing
And I wait for the light
To bring me home, while the radio plays

It's been oh so long!
Don't hold back tears
Darling –
Let the song come on

Pull the Curtain Closed

Swallowed by the breath of the wind
Swept away by the strength of the rain
Caught in circulations dust
Drifting misdirected through the plains
Where do questions go?
Where are the answered stowed?
In the lyrics of favourite songs
In the beauty of child's play
In the heartfelt confession
In the hurt of rage
The words unspoken
The future nightmares made
The dreams of some broken
Stories reclaimed –

So, answer old friend
Did you miss my smile?
Hear me old friend!
I miss yours
Did you fly for a while?
Out in the ether
And did you find your way back home?
You live in my dreams
In the broken seams
Of the fabrics your hands once stitched
But now they are ripped
And the tatters are caught
On the wires of the past
That won't let go
Oh, they won't let go!

Time

How does time feel
When you've forgotten timeless times?

The dust circling in the breeze
Filled with ashes from memories
Of souls that forgot the things
That I have too

Their stolen minds like a shell
Broken to pieces on scattered beach
Crushed by the most virulent waves
That don't see innocence
But say reach

Reach for the stars
Traverse to the safest heavens
For love of remembrance and warmth –
And trickle a tear
Down a faded wrinkled cheek

Footsteps on old roads
Replaced by footsteps in the trees
Swinging branch to branch
Until one breaks with me
And finally, I can see, again

I see my friends, I see my loves
Playing wilfully in the skies above
Daring me to laugh along with them
To forage my own path and pretend
That happiness is just a lonely song away

Dyson Russell

Standing idly at an open door
Yelling in a voice never heard before
Unfamiliar, yet begging to be let inside
To strangers I don't recognise
As they softly say my name

They say my name again
And in tears I pretend
To know them...

The door opens a little more wide
And the gorgeous light inside
Is so bright
I want to follow
In happy tears tonight

And I march into the most beautiful glow
Seeing fuzzy faces
I so desperately want to know
Looking back at all the seeds I've planted
But praying they never grow
Into the stolid heavy chains
That became my futile restraints
In tomorrow's yesterdays...

The Elephant

The rusted sound of the driest tears
Touching, scraping, down aged cheek
Leading to bygone memories lost creek
Forgotten by trampled paths left behind
But in the magic of fallen mind
From backstreets deserted and denied
Simple memories still spill teardrops –
And the once plentiful creek still flows
The shallow stream to laughter grows
Into gushing wakes of notions
From the gentle happy days

Tomorrow in Tomorrow

Blissful –
The ratty broken-down stars
Fall into perfect pieces
Cuts touch the brave
Dirt in mournful fingers
Luck in shallow graves
Of the fallen bruised
And the wildflower
That speaks in tongues
Across the harbour
In tune with disguises
In lofty wings
Sings, the song
Of serenity's arms
Belief is a charm
To slay tomorrow
Tomorrow

Four Leaf Clover

In the pastures green as spring
Are the secrets of our unity
Dust in bones
But strongest hands
As blinking fists make
Grains of sand
In a blind man's eyes

The seraphim slings arrows
To boldly pierce our spirits
While ghosts bleed on the train
And mindless thoughts
Submerged in rivers from tears cried
Don't feel the same, anymore –

Watching on the eyes of the skies
In the backstreets denied
And beating hearts intertwined

In rippling tears all that is held
In wrinkled hands all is felt, and touch dispelled
Black like fear, but darkness corrects
A finger to lips, and hair to caress

With nobility of words in songs that sparkle
In bottles of liquid that chase
Debacle... a word leaked from frowned faces
Dripping into lakes that I ignored
In friends
That left on a shooting star
To kingdom come, not my kingdom come...

Dyson Russell

An unknown creature lingers furtively –
- A paintbrush in his hand
With reverence, but conceit, he moistly paints
The withered masterpiece of his fate
Howling in bewilderment at a crescent moon
As bypassing strangers howl at it too
Crossing our view, used and subsumed

It's where he belongs –
In the far-out land, and on the distant breeze
To row in a paddle boat on ancient seas
While the piano thuds ballads of fear
And the sunset watches hapless spirit

All he asks for is heaven's halo
As dreamland becomes realities twin
Sickness in his body and soul –
The owl at midnight closes its eyes
His slit wrists bleeding
As the young man dies...
And the owl at midnight
Becomes the traveller wise

Bathed in sunshine, birds take flight
The lake with monsters, no, no, no
A Ferris wheel as patient as the day's memory
And the light still shines...

In an archaic palace from younger days
The flute played softly
Gifting children their wings
Broken, restrained

But even wings of paper can learn to repair
Wet or dry, high tides or cries
Wings of starships and written demise

Hallways laughing at every step
As locks bind tightly –
In a second is years
And years held in a breath
To touch with grace the secret codes
Love all that is left
In the days night time –

Like a journey not written
But a life in writing
To never fear the pied piper's tune
But play along with all that is true

On a voyage journeyed on older seas
And learned ears wise from different speech
To kingdom come, our kingdom come
But not yet reached

With sand that holds down everything
In oceans of tide, in rivers unwind
Plucked by the strings that spiders denied
From gutters deserted by the stars
Who we're looking for is who we are
When we walk on the path, we no longer know
And in its insanity the path asks the question
'Are you brave enough to stay?'

To catch the sun in a moment
And climb to the edge of darkness
And wonder why –

Where prayers scar your door
Blood marked by fables tomb
A famer ploughs the land
As the bull watches from afar
And like a harvest comes...

The villains taste their wine
And the serpents bite their tongues
The lovers ask to dance
As bells sound in the dark
We're happy with it all
Until day time runs
Out for good –

But a cure is never far
Because in a scar
Is who you are...

So let that rainbow trickle
Chase its every fever
Taste the fortunes of Eden
And the garden where bliss is found

A serpent can't deceive forever
And the last remaining soldier
Of a war fought together
Will never be lost
Unlike winter frost
On the distant sun –

As dragons run in search of sleep
And prophets laugh at fool's beliefs
Feet that never walked on soil
The ancient times
Modern man's spoil

And their dreams of antiquated travels
But a kingdom come, and now a kingdom unravelled
Stunning with magic, but no tricks to show
As air holds still, and deceit invents itself

While in the middle of it all
The vinyl still spins
The valentines stay tranquil
And the four-leaf clover sings
The sirens still call, and the drowned lives pretend
They're still all in one, so it'll never end...

With one last card to lay down
One last dice to throw around
A puzzle looks gainfully for its last piece
And their troubles make it ours
So please,
Fill the bottle as the bottle fills
And the water rushes for urgency laughs –

Running past a man on the land
With plants touching his feet
And sleepless laughter on repeat
It's finally where we belong!

In this sphere, a vision lived
Never paused, to forgive
A memory made from future tears
A future made from memories fears
Shaping the direction of the path
The very one that dared to ask
'Are you brave enough to stay?'

For the truth of the journey for these men
Lies not merely at the end
But in the footsteps walked on land in between
In the magical paintings and whimsical dreams
In the fabrics stitched from memories reached
To be the drum that forever beats

And having heard that majestic sound
Walked in unison on that ground
I would stand idly on that path forever
If it meant we could always stand together

I would burn down the sun
And water the skies
Hold onto the wind
And tell all the truths lies
Walk on the mountains green
And see the lamb be slain
I'd do it trapped in time
Again, and again...

Because in a paddock where one four leaf clover grows
I see three men, three men that I know
We wander together, not searching for cause
We wander together, and that's our reward
No sirens, no ambulances, though lights do shine
The four-leaf clover sings ever line

And when flags are flown
And lion hearts beat
In tune with flags with red stripes, white, and blue
A second could tick forever its true...

A broken poem, but not a broken pearl
A goddess in spirit, but not a girl

A new white line in a story not told
Writings on the wall, but their pictures are old
Never having searched for an answer at all
But the answer having searched for our question to call –

And now we count to four and say the names
Of the four-leaf clover, as it grows in rains
And we cry the tears that are the way back home
Our laughter the music to heaven's heaven
In the puzzle that found its last piece we're granted
The kingdom of our kingdom come

What Silky Hands Cannot Hold

Wrinkled faces
Golden fireflies and stunning heavens
In the wounded stars and tortured moons
I walk into honest memories
We unknowingly forgot to remember
Incense burns pungently like fires crackle
With silky hands holding on to smoke clouds
As we fly weightlessly into ocean blue, yet pale sky
Say after me – 'we know we're free'
In the sensual movements of woken daydream
In the fragments of footsteps, dust to remember
Winds, parsimonious, blow to speak
Of all the times we once had to lose
With thoughts forgotten held in fragile fists
And lovers joined by nascent hips
A second chance but a notion
Without will to fight for itself

The Last Poem

Born into loss, on whim
Ageless in death, a win
With golden memories
Seemingly in tact
Returning broken down
To the humblest Earth
With dust and debris and all that's left
Without the anguish of sentient mind
But to float in the ether
Through the backstreets, unwind
As lazy particles of the gentlest dust
As gorgeous ash, serene in windblow
Patiently, uncomplainingly, a mere atom, for eternity
As the happy minerals grow, together once again
Without conscious thought or fear
But with energy enough
To gift a river a tear
For nothing was ever born, or even started
It always was there
And will forever continue
In daydream
In peace –

Printed in the USA
CPSIA information can be obtained
at www.ICGtesting.com
LVHW101036100823
754634LV00009B/778